Adventures of Anansi and Sewa:
The Missing Black Panther

Written by Bunmi Oyinsan, PhD
Illustrated by Natalia Cano

Published by Nurturingminds.com (Nana Daycare)
https://nanadaycare.org/
Bowmanville, Ontario, Canada
Copyright Bunmi Oyinsan 2020

All rights reserved. No part of this publication may be reproduced, stored in a retrieval system, or transmitted in any form or by any means, electronic, mechanical, photocopying, recording or otherwise, without the prior consent of the copyright owner.

This book is sold subject to the condition that it shall not by way of trade or otherwise, be lent, resold, hired out or otherwise circulated without the copyright owner's prior consent in any form of binding or cover other than that which it is published and without a similar condition including this condition being imposed on subsequent purchaser.

ISBN 978-1-7772182-9-4

Dedicated to my grandchildren

It was a Friday night and Anansi had lost sight of his favorite toy. Anansi looked up and then he looked down, he searched his room but his favorite toy was nowhere to be found. Anansi stood in his room trying to think where his Black Panther could have gone.

He then went into Sewa's room. He opened her drawers, checked under the bed and in her closet. To his surprise he didn't find it.

Just as he was about to leave the room he saw a clenched fist sticking out from under Sewa's pillow. He picked up the pillow and there was his super hero!

It was his Black Panther dressed in a tutu! Sewa had dressed him in a skirt. Anansi was very angry and hurt so he stomped off to tell his parents.

"Mum! Sewa took my Black Panther! She took it out of my room and didn't even ask me. She put my Black Panther in a frilly skirt and made him look silly."

Sewa started to cry and her parents asked why she took Anansi's toy. "He never lets me play with his toys, it's just a doll and I wanted to play with it. He doesn't look silly just because he's wearing a tutu." Daddy Spider agreed with Sewa. He looked sternly at Anansi and said, "Your sister is right Anansi."

"He's not a doll, he is a superhero who is very strong and tall. How dare you call him a doll?" Anansi said and started stomping out of the room still angry. "My dolls are strong too!" Sewa said still crying.

Mummy Spider and Daddy Spider tried to console Sewa. "I share my toys, but he doesn't share his with me."

"I have and idea" Daddy Spider said as a smile lit up his face. "Let's play a game of hide and seek!" he tickled Sewa and laughter filled the whole place. "Go on then," said Mummy Spider to Sewa, "you be the first to hide. We will try and find you."

Sewa ran down the hallway still giggling, looking for a place to hide.

Anansi heard them giggling and wanted to be part of the game. He walked out of his room to the hallway to see what was going on.

"You can't join us! You've been mean to me all day." Sewa said. "I'm sorry Sewa, I want to play too!" Anansi said. He was already feeling bad for being so mean to Sewa.

You should not have been so hard on your sister for playing with your toy," said Mummy Spider who heard Anansi when he said sorry. "And Sewa, you should have asked your brother before taking his toy."

"I'm sorry Anansi," said Sewa.

"Anansi, you should always share," said Daddy Spider.

"That's true," said Mummy Spider. "It's important to share your toys and be a good example for your sister."

"Friends again?" Daddy Spider asked. Sewa and Anansi hugged. They had forgiven each other and were ready to play together.

They decided to play hide and seek with a little twist.

"Whoever finds the other person gets to hold the Black Panther when it's their turn to hide." Sewa suggested and Anansi thought it was a great idea.

The Black Panther ended up saving their day!

THE END

www.ingramcontent.com/pod-product-compliance
Lightning Source LLC
Chambersburg PA
CBHW040109120526
44589CB00040B/2834